LAURENCE KING

Published in 2017
by Laurence King Publishing Ltd
361–373 City Road
London EC1V 1LR
T: +44 20 7841 6900
F: +44 20 7841 6910
email: enquiries@laurenceking.com
www.laurenceking.com

This English edition was published by arrangement
with Albin Michel Jeunesse, Paris, France.

Copyright © 2016, Albin Michel Jeunesse
Original title: *La Coccinelle*

A catalogue record for this book is available
from the British Library.

ISBN: 978 1 78627 001 6

Printed in China, November 2016

The Ladybird

Bernadette Gervais

Laurence King Publishing

Actual size

Description

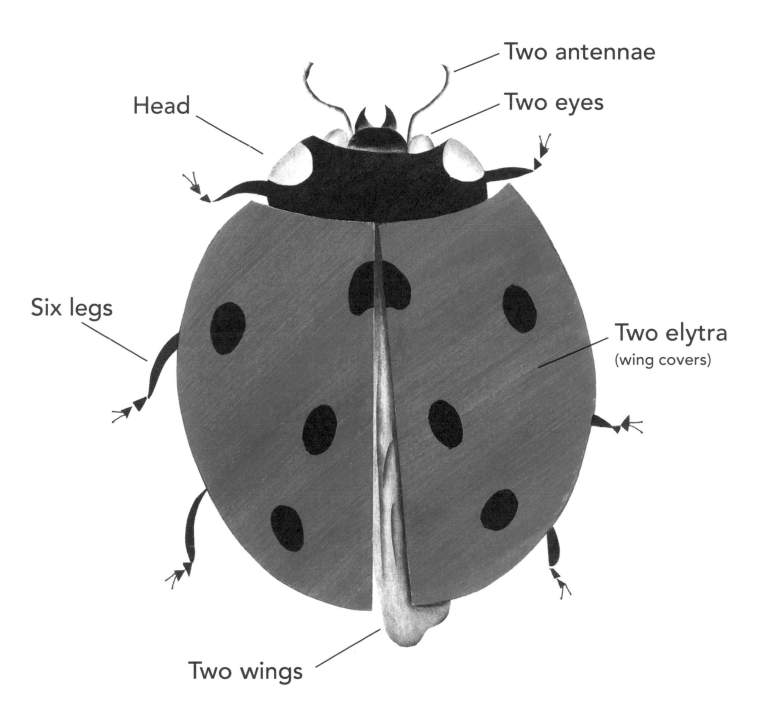

Two antennae

Two eyes

Head

Six legs

Two elytra
(wing covers)

Two wings

The legs

The ladybird can walk upside down thanks to small hooks on its legs.

The wings

To fly, the ladybird spreads its two red wing covers called elytra ...

The ladybird can fly up to a height of 2,000 metres (2 kilometres).

Means of defence

The ladybird plays dead to defend itself.
It lies on its back and folds in its legs ...

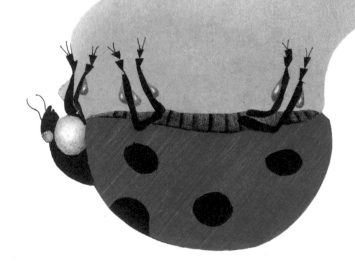

... or it lies on its back and releases a very bad smelling liquid from its legs to frighten off its enemies, birds.

Nutrition

The ladybird mainly eats small insects called aphids.
It can eat more than 50 a day.

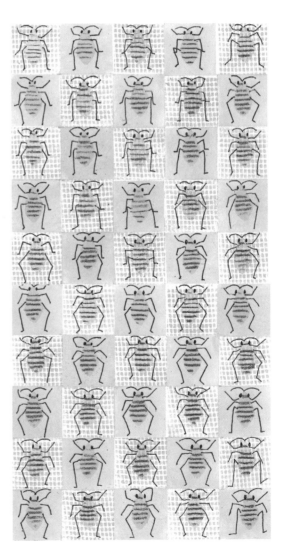

Hibernation

At the end of summer, dozens
of ladybirds gather together
and look for a safe place
to spend the winter.

Reproduction

In the spring,
after mating ...

It lays its eggs in
groups of 50.

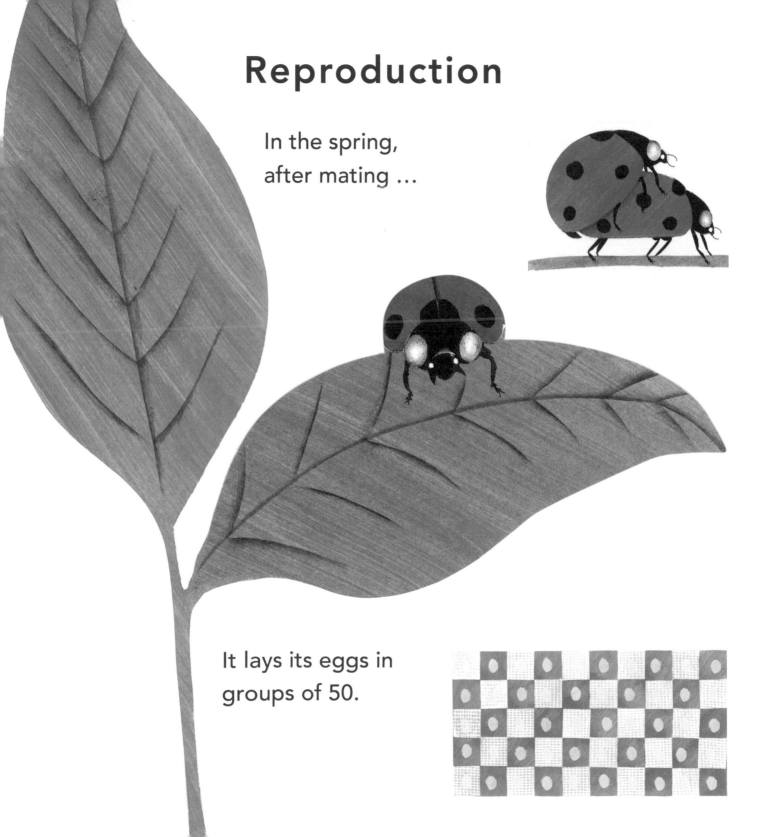

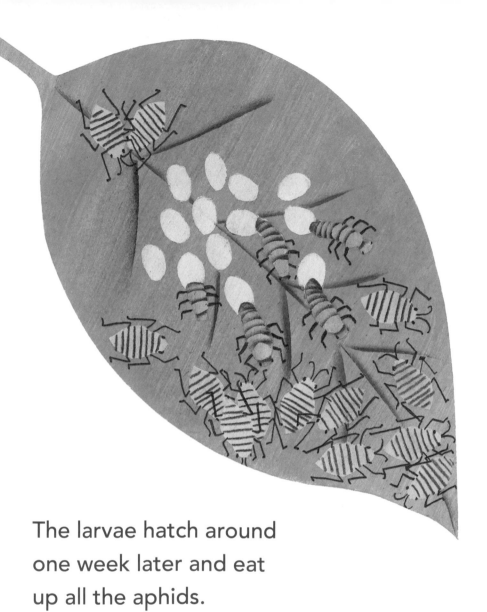

The larvae hatch around one week later and eat up all the aphids.

The larvae grow bigger and bigger.

The larva clings to a leaf.

At birth, the ladybird's elytra are soft and yellow.

As the ladybird grows older, its colour darkens.

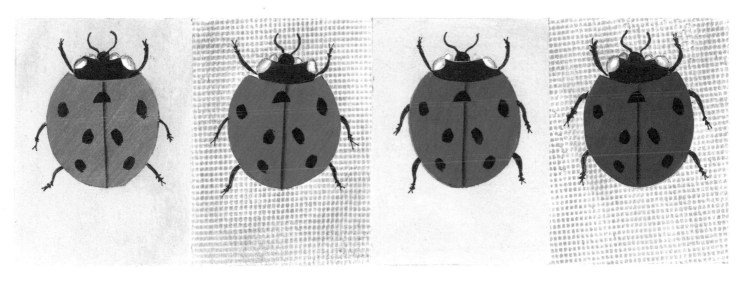

There are ladybirds with

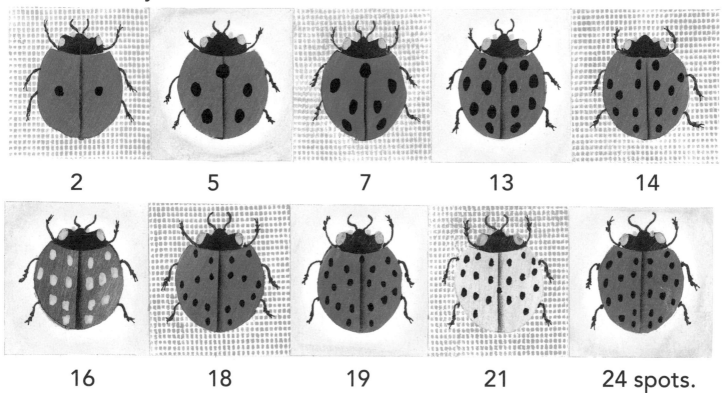

2   5   7   13   14

16   18   19   21   24 spots.

Here are some different types of ladybirds ...

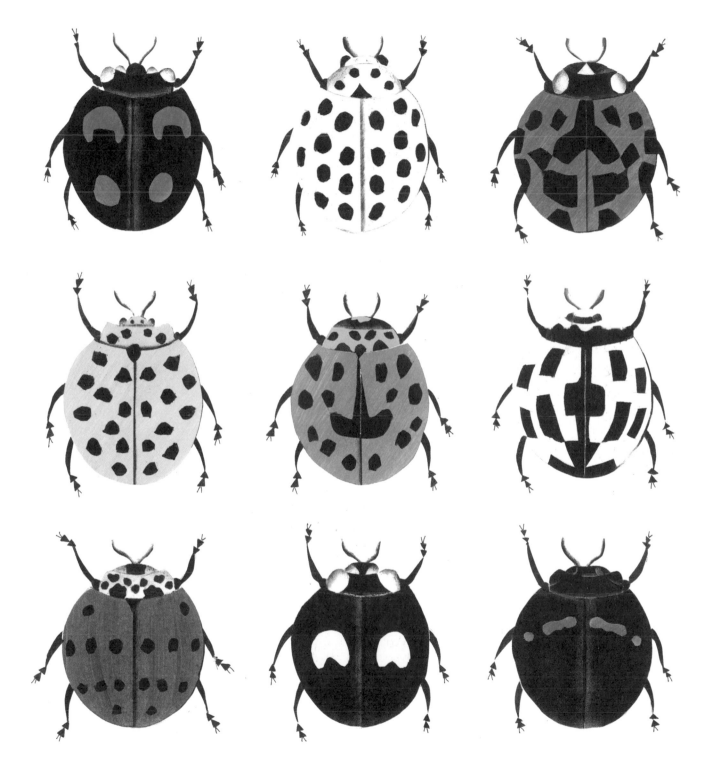

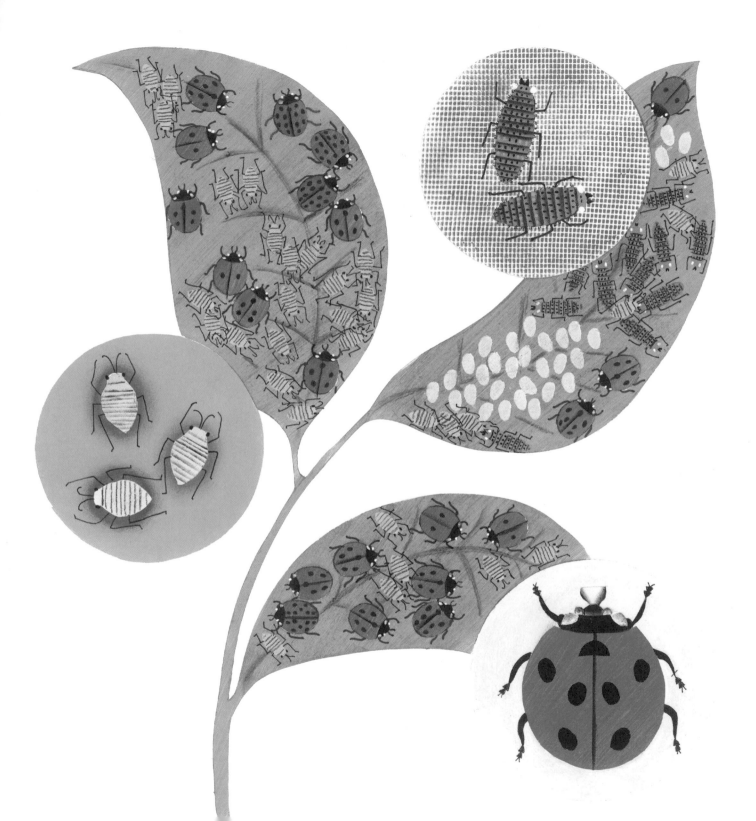

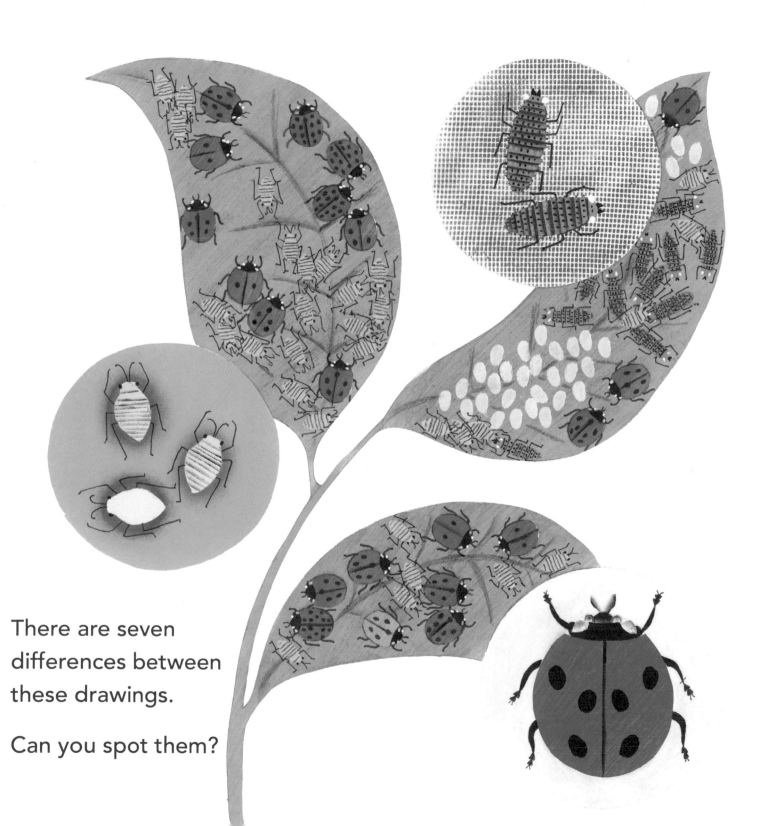

There are seven differences between these drawings.

Can you spot them?